# The Money Book

## A smart kid's guide to savvy saving and spending

by Elaine Wyatt and Stan Hinden • illustrated by Arnie Levin

**Tambourine Books**  **New York**

A SOMERVILLE HOUSE BOOK

Library of Congress Cataloging in Publication Data

Wyatt, Elaine. The money book and bank/by Elaine
Wyatt and Stan Hinden: illustrations by Arnie Levin p.
cm.
Summary: An introduction to money, how to budget
and save, banks and banking, shopping, and other
aspects of personal finance. Includes instructions for a
variety of projects such as making a savings bank.
1. Finance—Juvenile literature. 2. Finance, Personal—
Juvenile literature. 3. Money—Juvenile literature. 4.
Money-making projects for children—Juvenile
literature. 5. Economics—Juvenile literature. 1.
Finance, Personal. 2. Money. I. Hinden, Stan. II.
Levin, Arnie. III. Title.
HG173.8.W93 1991 332.024 — dc20 91-13237 CIP AC
ISBN 0-688-10365-010 9 8 7 6 5 4 3 2 1
First edition
A Somerville House Book
1 Eglinton Avenue East, Suite 305
Toronto, Ontario M4P 3A1
Printed in Hong Kong
Grateful acknowledgement is made to the following
copyright holders for permission to use material
contained in this book:
    page 10: material under head "Hats for Bread" is
reproduced from the *Money in Your Life* teacher
resource, published by The Canadian Bankers'
Association.
    page 53: statistics about lotteries used with
permission of *Gaming and Wagering Business*, New
York, N.Y.
    page 53: uneven odds used with permission of the
Crown Publishing Group, taken from *What are the
Chances? Risks, Odds, and Likelihood in Everyday Life*,
Crown Publishers Inc., New York, N.Y.

# CONTENTS

# Money, Money, Money

**Y**ou need money to buy an ice-cream cone. You have to put coins into a fare box when you climb aboard a bus. You must pay to get into the movies. You have to have cash to buy lunch at school. And you have to dig even deeper into your pockets to buy toys, books, tapes, or clothes.

LEMONADE
25¢ · 50¢

Money! It's just bits of metal and paper. But what would our lives be like without it? Money makes it possible to play video games or save for a new bike. Grown-ups also use money to buy groceries and to pay the rent.

Money is a serious matter. But if you understand it, then it will be easier for you to use it wisely.

As you read through this book, you'll learn how to earn money, how to take care of it, and how to spend it — all the skills that will help you be a savvy saver and spender the rest of your life.

FARE
$1.00

# The Hideaway Bank

he bank that comes with this book is the perfect place to keep your money — whether it is cash you earn, or money you get as gifts, or your allowance. Since the bank looks like a book, you can tuck it on your bookshelf among your books. Then only you will know where your money is hidden!

*Put your pennies in one slot, nickels in the next, then dimes, quarters, and finally fifty-cent pieces or dollars in the last slot. By counting up how many coins you have, you will know how much money you have saved.*

# Money and me

**W**hen you were little and went shopping with your mom and dad, you were probably given a few coins to spend as you liked. Perhaps you stood before jars filled with bubble gum, jelly beans, toffee, gumdrops, peppermint sticks, and chocolates, unable to decide which treat to buy. Remember how hard it was to make up your mind what to spend your money on?

Very few people have all the money they want. Most of us have to make choices. If we choose to do or buy one thing, it usually means we can't afford to do or buy something else.

If you had to make a choice, would you rather have skates or a bike, a book or a box of crayons, a hockey stick or a baseball cap, a licorice rope or a jump rope, a pet mouse or a doll house?

# Your Wish List

Make a list of all the things you'd like to buy or do.

Now, ask a grown-up to help you figure out what each one would cost. You might have to look in catalogs or visit some stores to find all the answers.

Study your list. Then imagine you had ten dollars. What would you buy? What if you had twenty dollars? One hundred dollars?

Everybody's answers will be different. If you feel your world would be empty without a puppy, you'll probably be willing to spend money on its care. If your friend is an avid drawer, he will want to spend his money on pencils and paper. Another friend might decide that she is willing to give up all her snacks to save for a baseball bat.

Bike $125.00
Crayons $5.00
Puppy $75.00
walkman $68.00

9

# Funny Money

**W**hat would you do if you wanted to buy an ice-cream cone but didn't have any money? You could make the ice cream yourself. But what if you didn't even have money to buy the cream and sugar? If you lived on a farm, you could get milk from a cow and trade some of it for the sugar.

For centuries, that's just what people did. They raised animals and tended gardens for their food, built their own homes and made their own clothing. When they needed something other people had, they traded — perhaps a bag of potatoes for some wool, a barrel of apples for nails.

Sometimes it was difficult to trade. People didn't always have what the other person wanted.

## Hats for Bread

Trading, or bartering, can be very difficult. Just imagine: A baker has bread and wants a toy for her child. A farmer has corn and needs meat. The toy maker has toys and needs some corn. The hunter has meat and wants a hat. The hatmaker has hats and wants some bread. So, he hurries off to the baker. The baker doesn't want his hats! How many trades will the hatmaker have to make to get the bread he wants?

(Answer on page 64.)

And a bag of potatoes was too heavy to carry around. Money helped solve these problems.

The first money wasn't coins or paper bills. Sometimes it was something rare or beautiful, like the teeth of whales or sharks, or shells, or feathers. Sometimes it was something useful, like salt, tools, nails, or furs.

Anything can be money — braids of elephant hair, bricks of tea, even the feathered skins of woodpeckers' heads — as long as people agree it is money. Money isn't just a thing, it's also an idea.

## Stone Broke

The money on the island of Yap in the Pacific Ocean was stone wheels carved from rock from the Belau Islands, three hundred miles across the ocean. The rock had to be carried to Yap by raft and often broke while being carved. Some wheels were larger than an elephant.

# WILL THAT BE ONE LUMP OR TWO?

Money makes life simpler, but it creates a strange problem. How do you get people to agree that something *is* money? Well, to begin with, it should be difficult to make or find, so that people can be sure it is real money. And it should be easy to carry around, so people can take it to the market.

Thousands of years ago, people began to use lumps of metal as money. Gold, silver, and copper were often chosen because they were rare, they were hard to fake, and they were soft enough to shape into small lumps.

But they were still awkward to use! Storekeepers had to keep scales to weigh the lumps brought to them. And customers didn't always trust the scales.

Around seven hundred years before the birth of Christ, the King of Lydia in Asia Minor, where Turkey is now, invented coins.

He molded lumps of metal into bean shapes, weighed each of them carefully, and marked them with the images of bulls and lions to tell his people how much each coin weighed. People believed in the value of the coins because they carried the mark of the king.

*The Athenian Owl, minted nearly 2,500 years ago, had an owl, the symbol of Athens, on its face.*

*The Lydian stater—the first coin.*

The idea spread throughout the ancient world. Rulers rushed to make coins with the images of gods, goddesses, mythical animals, military victories, bountiful harvests, and themselves — any image that would enhance the trust people had in the coin.

# Paper Money

Unfortunately, it's much easier to lose a coin than a barrel of potatoes or a chicken! A coin can slip out a hole in your pocket or be stolen by a thief with nimble fingers. To keep their money safe, people began to leave it with a monastery, a bank, or a goldsmith. The banker gave the owner of the money a slip of paper on which was written the value of the coins that were being held.

This slip of paper was easier to carry than a stack of coins, but it was worth as much. As it passed from person to person, each would know that he or she could demand the coins from the bank just by handing over the *bank note*.

People traveling between cities were especially worried about robbers along the country roads. Instead of carrying coins, these people had *letters of credit* from their banker asking the banker in the faraway city to give them money. These letters and notes are the ancestors of our modern paper money.

## Big Bucks

The Chinese were using paper money when Marco Polo, a famous Venetian trader, visited their country more than six hundred years ago. As early as 1275 A.D., the Chinese Emperor Kublai Khan stamped sheets of black mulberry paper with his red seal. The paper money was large, about the size of a page in a school workbook, and carried the stern warning that anyone caught making fake money would have his or her head chopped off.

# MONEY OF THE NEW WORLD

In the early days of the New World, France and England sent only a few coins to the colonists. And those coins that were sent were often lost when the ships carrying them sank in storms.

Since coins were scarce, pioneers used other things as their money — nails, gunpowder, fishhooks, bullets, furs, and tobacco. Money was so rare in colonial Canada that in 1685 the governor was unable to pay the soldiers protecting the colonists. Rather than wait for a shipment of coins from France, he dripped wax on the back of playing cards, stamped the cards with his seal, and signed them. He used the

playing-card money to pay the soldiers, merchants, and clerks. Different values were given to the cards by clipping their corners or cutting them in half or quarters. Playing-card money was used in Canada for seventy-five years — until 1759.

## JOACHIMSTHALERS

Many years ago, before the discovery of America, there were hundreds of different kinds of coins in Europe — so many that people were easily cheated. Then, around the time Christopher Columbus was searching for new lands, a man called Count Schlick began to make coins out of the silver from a mine near St. Joachimsthal in Bohemia. The coins were well made and were soon trusted across Europe. They were originally called Joachimsthalers (say "Yo-ah-kims-tah-ler"), but people soon began calling them "thalers" for short. In different countries, "thaler" became "reichsthaler" (Germany), "rigsdaler" (Scandinavia), "rijksdaalder" (Holland), and finally "dollar."

## The Pine Tree Shilling

Desperate for real money yet forbidden by England to make coins, the Massachusetts Bay Colony built a secret mint in Boston in 1652. The Boston coins had the images of willow, oak, and pine trees and the word "masathusets." The colonists struck their "pine tree shillings" for thirty years — each coin dated 1652 to fool the British.

## Two Bits

Another silver coin trusted by people across Europe was the Spanish "piece of eight," worth eight reals. Merchants and sailors carried the coin to the Americas, where it became known as the Spanish dollar. It was soft, and if you wanted to make change, you could chop the coin in half and then into quarters. Half was called "four bits" and a quarter was called "two bits."

# The Making of Money

Coins are made in a place called a mint. In the old days, these were hot, dirty places. The noise of hammering and pounding was deafening. Fire-spitting furnaces heated metal, while horses in harnesses drove the machines that flattened the hot metal into sheets and punched out blank coins. Men fed these coins by hand into machines that pounded the designs on them.

## A Mint a Minute

In 1793, the United States' first mint, founded in Philadelphia, produced 11,178 copper cents — fewer than 31 coins a day, and fewer coins than the mint can make in a minute today. In fact, today's machines can make as many as 1,000 pennies a second.

1793     TODAY

Today, coins are still made by heating metal and pressing it into thin sheets. A machine cuts out blank coins, just as a cookie cutter cuts out cookies. These blanks fall into a machine that makes rims on their edges.

Finally, the design is pounded into the coins just as it was in the olden days.

## Your Own Mint

If you invented your own currency, what would you call it? What would it look like?

You can make your own coins by rolling out clay or dough, then cutting out coins using a thimble or small jar. Press or draw designs into your coins before letting them dry.

Dough for Dough

1 cup flour
2 tablespoons salt
2 tablespoons oil
1/4 cup water

Combine flour, salt, and oil. Add water slowly while stirring. You may need more water. Knead dough until smooth.

# FAKE MONEY

No sooner were coins invented than dishonest people found a way to cheat others. Some crooks would copy a design and make coins from cheaper metals, like lead. Other people cheated by scraping slivers of gold or silver from the edges of coins. Early coins had strange shapes — it was hard to make them round — and they didn't have the ridged edges that coins have today. If the crook took only a little, the coin didn't look very different than it had before it was clipped.

Modern crooks rarely bother to make fake coins. They prefer to make fake dollar bills. To discourage these criminals — called counterfeiters — governments try to make it tough to copy their paper money. They cover the bills in swirls and curlicues and intricate drawings of buildings, people, animals, and flowers. Some of the images are carved deep into steel plates that leave a thick layer of ink on the paper, which you can feel when you run your finger over a

bill, unless it is very old and worn.

The paper, too, is special. In the United States, the paper on which dollar bills are printed is made of linen and cotton with small fibers of red and blue silk. Canadian money is made of cotton with

## Worthless Wampum

Crooks even made fake wampum. Wampum was purple and white shells carved into beads and strung into belts or bracelets by Native Americans. The early Dutch and English settlers had so few coins that they used wampum as money. It became worthless after a settler began producing porcelain wampum at a factory in New Jersey in 1760.

small green disks, called planchets, scattered throughout the bills. Canadian $50 and $100 bills also have a small, dark patch in the corner. The patch is about the size of your fingernail and

changes from green to gold as you move the bill back and forth. British money has a ribbon of invisible metallic thread that conducts electricity in a special way.

## Can You Spot a Fake?

Would you like to help the police find counterfeit money? To be able to recognize a fake bill, you have to know what a real one looks like. Most counterfeit bills can be spotted because the lines are smudged.

Look at a bill through a magnifying glass. See how fine the lines are.

*Here's a game for you to play. Can you find the mistakes we made on these bills?*

# Making Allowances

**A**llowances!
    Do you get an allowance each week? Do your friends? Do you think you get enough? Your parents probably give you an allowance so you'll learn to handle money wisely and grow up to be a smart spender and saver.

# Money Talks

Whether you get an allowance now, or just hope to get one soon, sit down with your parents and discuss what it means to all of you.

Here are some questions you might like to ask. There are no right or wrong answers, but see if you and your parents can agree on what answers are right for your family.

- How much will I get?
- What things will I be expected to buy with my allowance?
- How often will I receive it?
- Do I have to do any work for it? If so, what chores do I have to do?
- What happens if I don't do my chores?
- Can I do extra chores to earn a bit more?
- What kind of chores? How much will I get?
- Do I have to save some of my allowance?
- Can I spend the rest of it as I like?

# EXTRA CHORES

Almost all kids are expected to do their share of household chores. They empty wastebaskets, vacuum, dust, take the garbage out, set and clear the table, go to the store for milk, wash or dry the dishes, feed the hamster, and keep their rooms tidy. Some kids iron clothes, wash cars, or cook meals.

Some parents are willing to pay for special jobs like cleaning out the garage or washing windows. If your parents agree to pay you for work, try to be businesslike. Agree ahead of time what the job is and how much money you'll be paid. And promise to do the job by a certain time or on a certain day.

## HOW TO EARN MONEY AROUND THE HOUSE

| Task | How much will you be paid? | When will you do the job? |
| --- | --- | --- |
| | | |

# Making Money

**T**here's nothing like the sound of money you've earned jingling in your jeans. Earning your own money gives you a feeling of independence and a sense of control over your life.

## What Can a Kid Do?

Some kids baby-sit. Others wash cars or mow lawns. But these aren't the only jobs you can do. There are all kinds of ways to earn money. You can make and sell things like jewelry, kites, hats, or origami decorations. People often buy objects that are unique and can't be bought in stores.

You can also do work that people don't have time, or don't want, to do themselves. Kids look after their neighbors' pets, or they shovel snow, weed gardens, or rake leaves. Some deliver flyers or newspapers. Kids who have learned magic tricks or juggling sometimes get jobs as magicians or clowns at parties. You can collect worms in your own backyard and sell them to people who like to fish.

Almost any kind of work is more satisfying — and pays better — if you turn it into a business. Rather than pulling weeds or mowing a lawn just once in a while, you could agree to tend a yard for an entire season. You might promise to mow the lawn once a week, water the grass when it is dry, dig out weeds as soon as they sprout, and rake the leaves in the fall.

You could agree to keep a neighbor's walk and driveway clear of snow for the whole winter. An offer to turn up with your shovel by 7:30 every snowy morning would be hard for anyone to refuse. Once you have a customer, you'll have to keep that promise, even on those cold, dark mornings when you'd rather snuggle into your blankets for another five minutes of sleep.

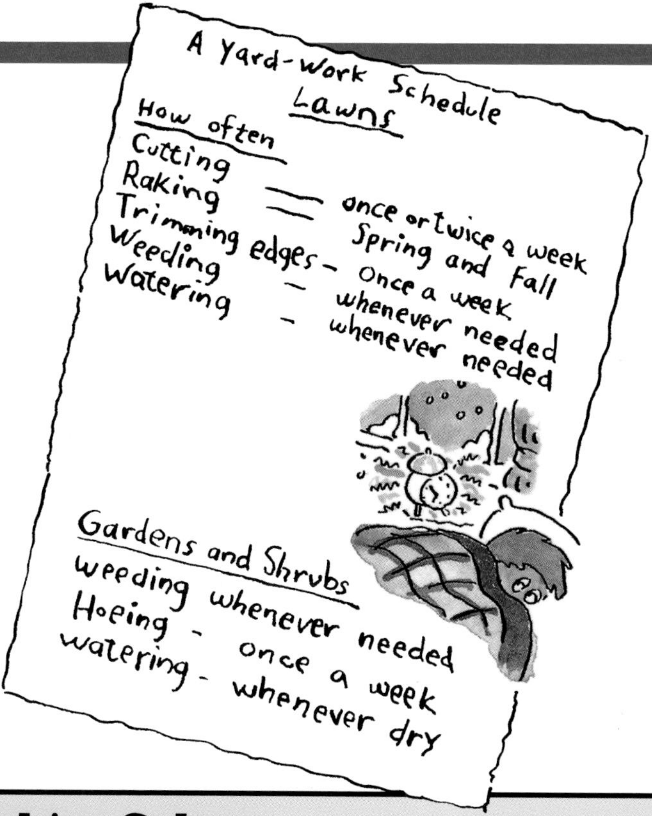

A Yard-Work Schedule

## Lawns

How often

Cutting
Raking     ── once or twice a week
Trimming edges ── Spring and Fall
Weeding    ── Once a week
Watering   ── whenever needed
           ── whenever needed

## Gardens and Shrubs

Weeding whenever needed
Hoeing ── once a week
Watering ── whenever dry

# Cookies Galore

Most adults like to buy things made by kids because they have a personal touch, unlike the machine-made things sold in stores. Kids will like the things you make if they're good to eat or fun to play with.

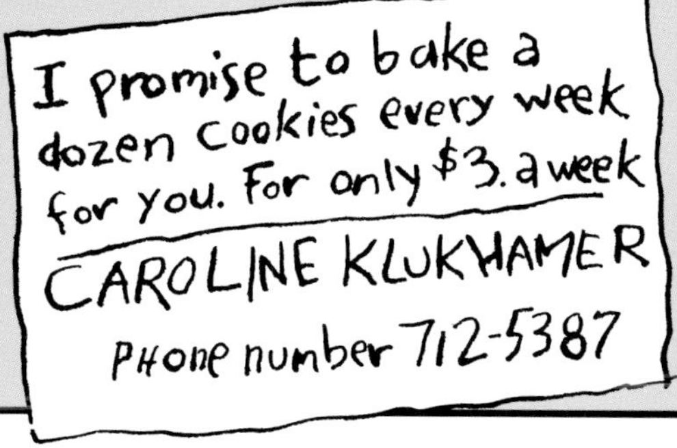

I promise to bake a dozen cookies every week for you. For only $3. a week

CAROLINE KLUKHAMER

PHONE number 712-5387

# The Neighborhood Can-do Kid

**W**ork isn't just a way to make money. It should be interesting — at least some of the time. What kind of job would you like to do? First, consider your interests and skills. Are you a good cook? Are you skilled at repairing bikes? Do you like animals? Do you enjoy being outside in a garden? Are you a whiz at origami or knitting? Perhaps you are a good teacher and could earn money by showing younger kids how to knit, or do magic tricks, or build model airplanes, or change a tire on a bicycle.

If you can't decide what you'd like to do, find out what your friends do, how much they get paid, and what they like about their work.

Ready to get to work? You'll have to decide how much to charge, and you'll have to let people know that you're in business. For some jobs, you'll need supplies or equipment. If you're going to clean basements, you'll need brooms, buckets, soap, and rags. If you're going to make cookies, you'll need sugar, flour, and other ingredients. Discuss with your parents what things you can use from home.

Before you begin working, give yourself time to build the skills you need to do your job well. Baby-sitters feel more confident if they have taken a course in baby-sitting and first aid. Some kids begin their baby-sitting careers by working as a mother's helper. Kids who wash cars, clean windows, or mow lawns usually get their experience working for their parents.

AL&BOBS GARAGES AND BASEMENTS CLEANED

**Jobs Most Often Done by Eight- to Thirteen-year-olds**

- Washing cars
- Household chores
- Raking leaves
- Shoveling snow
- Feeding pets
- Baby-sitting
- Mowing lawns
- Yard work
- Walking dogs
- Paper routes

# TAKE A DOG FOR A JOG

Kids and pets need each other, especially in the city.

Most city dogs, particularly dogs that live in apartment buildings, can't go out for a walk unless someone takes them. Pet owners often need someone to look after small animals while they're away on vacation. Birds, fish, gerbils, even iguanas need to be given food and fresh water. Cats need a scratch behind the ear and a game of chase-the-rumpled-paper-mouse.

If you want to be a dog walker, you'll need to let people know the days and times you're available. Tell them how long the dog will be walked. Most dog owners want their dog to be out for at least forty-five minutes.

Try to walk only one dog at a time, especially if you're walking big dogs. You could end up in a tangle, or the dogs might get in a fight. Always keep the dog on a leash. If you let it loose, you may not be able to get it back. Besides, if the dog just can't resist chasing cars, you could be risking its life.

Most cities and towns frown on pet owners who let their pets relieve themselves in the park or streets and don't clean up. Even if it's not your dog, you'll be expected to scoop up after the pet. So carry a pooper scooper.

If you are hired as a pet sitter by neighbors on vacation, try to become friends with the pet before the owner leaves. Be sure the pet owner tells you exactly what you'll have to do. Ask lots of questions:

- How often should I feed the pet?
- How much should I feed it? Where is the food kept?
- Do I need to clean the tank, cage, or litter box?
- Should I groom the dog or cat?
- When should the dog be walked? Is the cat allowed outside?
- What's the name and telephone number of the vet?
- When are the owners coming back?

# BABY-SITTING

Do you have lots of patience? Are you a bit of a clown? Can you make peanut butter sandwiches? Are you calm in a crisis? Yes? Maybe you should baby-sit.

The first job most baby-sitters get is playing with toddlers during the afternoon while the mother or father is busy in the house doing something else. As the parents get to know you, they'll feel comfortable leaving you alone with the children for an hour or so in the afternoon while they do some shopping. Before long, you'll be baby-sitting at night.

Whenever you look after a child, you'll be expected to keep the child happy as well as safe. It doesn't take much time or money to create a treasure sack that will keep a child busy for hours. If you have an old shopping bag handy, you can drop all sorts of junk into it for crafts: old magazines and used greeting cards for cutting up, old hats and jewelry for dressing up, worn socks and mittens for puppets, paper for drawing or folding into airplanes.

Buy a small record-keeping book and keep notes of every baby-sitting job you get. When someone calls, write down the date and time you're to baby-sit, the address, and the names and ages of the children. When you arrive to sit, have the parents write down the phone numbers of the family doctor, a neighbor, and where the parents will be while they're away. Ask if there are any special instructions. What time do the kids go to bed? Are they allowed to have a snack? May they watch TV? Do they have a special toy or blanket they take to bed?

# My Baby-sitting Checklist

Day and time of baby-sitting job

_____

Parents' names

_____

_____

Telephone number

_____

Address

_____

Names and ages of children

_____

_____

Phone numbers:  Family doctor _____

              Neighbor _____

              Emergency _____
Where will parents be

_____

_____

Special instructions

_____

_____

# DELIVERING NEWSPAPERS

Delivering newspapers is hard work, but it probably pays more than any other job for kids. Newspapers are heavy, and delivering the daily paper takes about an hour every day, rain or shine. You might have to get out of bed early in the morning or give up all your after-school activities. You may also have to spend a couple of hours every weekend collecting money for the papers.

Still interested? To get a paper route, call the circulation department of your local paper. They'll be able to tell you if you're old enough (you'll probably have to be at least ten years old) and how to apply. Once you've applied, you'll be interviewed by someone from the paper. If you get the job, you and your parents will be asked to sign a contract making certain promises.

# TURNING JUNK INTO MONEY

Yard sale, garage sale, tag sale. Whatever you call it, your parents will love it! The first thing you have to do is clean up your room. You might clean the basement, too.

Your old books, toys you've outgrown, and those clothes that don't fit — especially blue jeans — will be snatched up by other kids. You can sell jewelry, baseball cards, skates, magazines, comics, posters, and records.

Two hot items at yard sales are old records (or tapes) and magazines. Ask your friends to bring their old treasures as well. The more things you collect to sell, the more interesting your sale will be to browsers and buyers.

Clean everything, especially toys and clothes. No one will buy something that's dirty. Decide how much you should charge for each thing, then write the price on a tag and tape or tie it to the item.

The best time to have a garage sale is on a weekend, especially during the summer. Put up lots of posters advertising the date, time, and location of the sale. Make sure you have plenty of change. On a warm, sunny day you can boost your profits by setting up a lemonade stand for all the thirsty customers.

If you don't sell everything, don't be too disappointed. You can always try again next year. Or you can donate the unsold items to a charity.

# WANT WORK BUT NOT SURE HOW TO FIND IT?

The best way to find a job is to swallow your nervousness and talk to people. Ask your neighbors and friends and ask them to tell their friends. This is no time to be shy. Let everyone know that you'd like to baby-sit or walk a dog or rake leaves. Or you can ask people what work they need done. Does their basement need to be cleaned? Do they have old magazines or newspapers that should be tied up?

## Business Cents

Working can be lots of fun, but if you're not making a profit you're not going to be able to stay in business for very long. Your *profit* is the money you have left in your pocket after you've paid for the things you had to buy to do the job. To know whether you're making a profit, keep careful records, especially if you're making things to sell.

Buy a notebook to keep track of your business. On one page list all your *expenses* — the costs of

doing business. These include things like soaps and sponges, or flour and sugar. On the opposite page, keep track of your *revenue* — what you earn. Add up all your expenses and subtract them from the revenue. Whatever is left over is your profit.

RECORD-KEEPING BOOK

KATIE'S JEWELRY
Expenses for June

| | |
|---|---|
| Candy decorations | $3.60 |
| modeling clay | 6.00 |
| Plain barrettes | 4.30 |
| Brooch pins | 5.00 |
| Lacquer | 8.00 |
| Lacquer brushes | 1.25 |
| Total | $27.55 |

Revenues for June

Mrs Jones: 1 fruit brooch ($7.each) $7.00
June Fair:
   4 Gummi Bear barrettes ($4.each) 16.00
   2 pizza brooches ($3.each) 6.00
   1 hamburger tie pin ($3.each) 3.00
Melissa: Jelly-bean barrette ($6.each) 6.00
Joan: Jelly-bean barrette ($6.each) 6.00
      total $44.00

| | |
|---|---|
| Revenues | $ 44.00 |
| Expenses | −27.55 |
| Profit | $16.45 |

# Where Did All My Money Go?

**H**ave you ever wondered where all your money went? Just a few days ago you had lots — and now it's all gone! Have you ever bought something and then been sorry later?

What you need is a budget. A budget is a plan that will help you spend your money exactly the way you want.

## Your Spending Record

It's not hard to make a budget. Start by making a list of everything you spend your money on each week and how much each item costs.

| DAY | Items | Cost |
|-----|-------|------|
| MONDAY | | |
| TUESDAY | | |
| WEDNESDAY | | |
| THURSDAY | | |
| FRIDAY | | |
| SATURDAY | | |

At the end of a week, look over your spending diary. Are you spending more on snacks or baseball cards or soft drinks than you want to? Are you spending money simply because it's in your pocket? Do you buy things just because your friends buy them?

All of us have a few habits we don't like. Once you understand your spending habits, you'll find it easier to change them. As you reach for that bag of potato chips, think about it. Are you really hungry? Would you rather keep the quarters in your pocket? If you spend them now, you can't put them in your Hideaway Bank later.

# YOUR BUDGET

The second step in budgeting is to set a goal. Your goal can be simple — perhaps you want to save one dollar a week. Or you might want to save fifty dollars for a special purpose, like a Christmas gift or a summer outing. Having a goal and reaching it can be very satisfying.

## Saving for a Reason

What would you like to buy more than anything else?

_____

How much does it cost?
$_____

How much can you save each week or month?
$_____

How long will it take you to save enough to buy it?

_____

38

# Making Your Own Budget

Start with how much money you have each week — your allowance and any money you earn. Then subtract how much you plan to save. How much is left?

Now list how much you plan to spend on the things you need and want. A look at your spending diary on page 37 will help.

**My Budget**

| | |
|---|---|
| Weekly allowance and earnings | $_____ |
| Weekly savings | $_____ |
| Money left to spend | $_____ |

**Each week I plan to spend my money on:**

| | |
|---|---|
| Bus fare | $_____ |
| School lunches | $_____ |
| Snacks | $_____ |
| Books | $_____ |
| Magazines | $_____ |
| Comics | $_____ |
| Cassette tapes | $_____ |
| Movies | $_____ |
| Clothes | $_____ |
| Sports | $_____ |
| Hobbies | $_____ |
| Video games | $_____ |
| Other | |
| Total | $_____ |

# Money in the Bank

**$** 435,200,000,000! That's 435 billion 200 million U.S. dollars. It's a lot of money, and it's all in one bank — the Dai-Ichi Kangyo Bank Ltd. of Japan, the largest bank in the world.

Your neighborhood bank doesn't have nearly that much money, but it's still a safe place to keep your money. As soon as your Hideaway Bank is bulging with coins, you should think about opening a bank account.

There are lots of good reasons to keep your money in a bank. It will be safe there, because you can't lose it if it's in the bank. And you won't be as tempted to spend it.

What's more, your money will grow in the bank.

## Why Is Your Money Safe in a Bank?

Great precautions are taken to protect the money that people put in banks. Banks are heavily guarded, and bank employees are carefully screened for honesty. Finally, your money is protected by the federal deposit insurance corporation against loss or theft. Even if the bank is robbed or goes out of business, you will be given back your money.

In many banks, it's hard to spot the "guards." Take a look around next time you're in the bank and see if you can guess how the bank might catch a robber. (Hint: the "guards" in your bank might not be human beings, but they might still be able to "see.")

# How Does Your Money Grow?

A bank is a business, just like a restaurant or a store. The business of banks is to keep people's savings safe.

But a bank doesn't just put your money in a vault. It lends some of your money to other people. These people must pay back the money they borrow, plus a little bit more. The "little bit more" is called *interest.* Then the bank gives most of the interest your money has earned to you. That's how your money grows. It earns interest while it's in the bank.

## Money in the Bank

The word "bank" comes from the Italian word *b a n c a,* the bench at which the money changers sat in the marketplaces in Italy nearly five hundred years ago. A dishonest money changer had his bench broken — his *b a n c a* was *r o t t a.* That's how we got the word "bankrupt," which describes someone who has fallen deeply into debt.

## Money Doesn't Grow on Trees — It Grows in a Bank

8 years
7 years
6 years
5 years
4 years
3 years
2 years
1 year

Let's pretend you have $10 in the bank. The bank will say thanks by giving you interest on your money. If they give you 10¢ for $1 kept in the bank for a year, at the end of a year you'll have your original $10, plus $1 worth of interest. Your $10 becomes $11!

If you leave your money in the bank, it will begin to grow even faster. Now that you have $11, the bank will pay you $1.10 interest at the end of a year. Your $11 will become $12.10. The interest on $12.10 will be $1.21. And at the end of the third year, you'll have $12.10 plus $1.21 or $13.31.

How much will you have at the end of ten years? (Answer on page 64)

# CHECKING IT OUT

It's time to take all your money to the bank. Most kids put their money in a *savings account* — an account that will hold their money and pay interest every month or so. When you open an account, you'll be given a *passbook* with an

*A passbook*

*A withdrawal slip*

account number and be asked to sign your name on a piece of paper. In your passbook, the bank will record your *deposits,* which are the money you put into your account, and your *withdrawals,* which are the money you take out of your account.

You might want to pick a bank that has *automated teller machines*, which are sometimes called bank machines. These machines will let you deposit and withdraw money with a special plastic card even when the bank is

*A bank card*

your money safe. But when you want to take money out of your account, you don't have to go to the bank. Instead, you can write a *check*. Signing your name on a check is like writing a letter to the bank asking it to take money from your account and give it to the person named on the check.

closed. Instead of signing your name, you use a secret code called a *personal identification number*, or *PIN*.

A *checking account* isn't very different from a savings account. It, too, is a place to keep

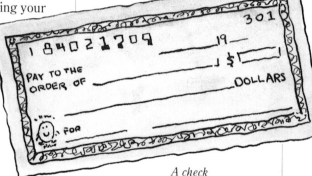
*A check*

## Signing Your Money Away

Practice your signature. Are you going to use your full name or just your initials? Try different styles before deciding on the one you like.

*Billy Bagwell*   *Billy Bagwell*   *Billy Bagwell*
*Billy Bagwell*   *Billy Bagwell*

# HELPING YOURSELF TO SAVE

Banking is simple. It's saving that is hard — especially when there are so many tempting things to spend your money on! Saving is a skill, and if you follow some of these tips you'll soon find the stacks of coins in your Hideaway Bank bursting through the top.

## Savings Tips

- It's easier to save if you have a goal. What do you want? A bike, some new clothes, a science set, a birthday present for your best friend?
- Don't carry any more money around than you need. If you don't have it in your pocket, you won't spend it.

- Remember your budget. Keep it up to date.
- Save first, not last. Put your savings in your Hideaway Bank as soon as you get your money. Don't try to save whatever is left at the end of the week. Most of the time there won't be any!

- Don't be afraid to be different. Some kids buy stuff just because their friends do. They usually end up broke. If your friends wonder why you are not buying things, tell them you're saving for something special.
- Start with a small goal. Set your sights on something you can buy within a few weeks. If it takes an eternity to save for the first special thing you want, you'll give up in frustration.
- Every once in a while, take your money out of your Hideaway Bank and count it. It can be very satisfying to watch your savings grow.

# Smart Shopping

**S**o far we have seen how you can get money (from your allowance and by working for it), and how you can make your own budget, and how you can save money. Now comes the part you have been saving for.

Let's go shopping!

But first let's see how you can be a smart shopper. Shopping wisely is a skill. It won't give you more money to spend, but it will boost your "purchasing power"— your ability to buy more with the money you have.

## Shopping Tips

Before you spend your money, ask yourself some questions.

- Do you really need this toy (or game or cassette tape)? Will you be bored with it tomorrow?
- Can you get it cheaper somewhere else? Different stores charge different prices for the same thing. If you are buying something big, like a guitar, or if you buy the same thing often — like food for your hamster — you can save money by shopping around. That means watching for sales in the newspapers, looking in catalogs, and phoning different stores to find the lowest prices.
- Do you know what you're buying? Always read the labels or packaging. They should tell you what the product will do, how it should be cared for, and how it should be used.
- Does it fit? Always try on clothing before taking it home.

# The Experts

Imagine you need new batteries. If you go to the store, you'll see lots of brands — some more expensive, some claiming to last longer. Which would you buy?

Since it isn't always possible to judge just by looking whether something is well made or worth the price, there are groups of people who test all kinds of things. You can read the results of their tests in magazines like *Zillions* and *Consumer Reports* in the United States and *Canadian Consumer* and *Protect Yourself* in Canada.

Here's a report on batteries like one you might find in a consumer magazine. It shows how long different batteries last and how much they cost for each hour of power.

Which batteries should you buy?

## BATTERY LIFE (HOURS)

| | 0 | 1 | 2 | 3 |
|---|---|---|---|---|
| Brightlast | | | | |
| Longlife | | | | |
| Everglow | | | | |

## COST (CENTS PER HOUR)

| | 0 | 1 | 2 | 3 | 4 |
|---|---|---|---|---|---|
| Brightlast | | | | | |
| Longlife | | | | | |
| Everglow | | | | | |

As you can see, Longlife lasts longer (almost two hours) and costs less. It would be the best buy. Brightlast lasts almost as long as Longlife but costs more. Everglow lasts less than an hour and costs the most.

# THE JINGLES THAT JANGLE

Here's a riddle: It lasts about thirty seconds but won't go away. What is it? A television commercial!

Commercials are made by people who want you to buy their brand of breakfast cereal or toothpaste or automobile. It's hard to ignore commercials, but if you know how they work to persuade you to buy, you'll be able to watch them with more understanding.

## Buy Me, Buy Me

Here are a few of the different kinds of commercials. Can you think of examples of each kind?

- The Fun-Fun-Fun Ad: These ads show happy people doing great things — skydiving, rafting, skiing, skate boarding, laughing with lots of friends. There are bright colors and flashing lights and exciting sounds. Do you believe that if you buy their product you'll be popular and have lots of fun, too?

- The Slice-of-Life Ad: These ads make you feel cozy. A grandpa and his grandson chat over a bowl of cereal, or sisters share memories during a long-distance telephone call. The advertisers try to link their product to moments in life when we feel content and secure. Do you think you'll feel secure if you buy their product?

- The Famous-Person Ad: Popular athletes and performers appear in some ads. Do

you want to buy a product just because someone famous tells you to?

- The Word-Game Ad: Advertisers love words like "new," "improved," "whiter," "cleaner," "richer," "softer." But do you think you can tell the difference?

- The Number-Game Ad: Ads tell us that four out of five doctors recommend a cough syrup or a headache tablet or a brand of diapers. Or they tell us that four out of five kids prefer Zippy Cola over Drippy Cola. Do you always like what everyone else likes?

- The Information Ad: Some commercials seem packed with facts, but they may not tell you all the facts you need to make a

sound decision. A fast-food restaurant might tell you that its burger is bigger than another burger, but might not tell you it also costs more. Other ads make a fuss about a certain ingredient — a special kind of fluoride in toothpaste or a whitener in a laundry detergent — without any proof that it's any better than the ingredients in competitors' products.

## Playing the Ad Game

While you watch television, see if you can spot the method the commercial is using to persuade you to buy the product. You might even find more than one trick in each ad. The star of an ad might be a popular singer who makes the product look like fun — this is a Famous-Person Ad combined with a Fun-Fun-Fun Ad. See if you can create new, improved ads to replace the ads that use tricks and games.

# Going into debt

**W**hat can you do if you want to buy something but you don't have the money? You can save your money until you have enough. Or you can borrow money from someone else.

Borrowing is serious because it is someone else's money you're spending. The person who has lent you the money will want it back.

Borrowing money means making a promise — the promise to return the money.

When people borrow money from a bank, they not only have to pay back the money they borrowed, they also have to pay an additional amount, called *interest.* If people borrow $100 from a bank, they might have to pay back $110 — the $100 borrowed plus $10 interest.

Borrowing makes it possible to buy the things we want now and to pay for them in the future. People

## IOUs

Imagine you are with your friends on a really hot day. Everyone else is buying an ice-cream cone, but you have no money in your pocket. Your friend is willing to lend you the money. You promise to pay the money back the next day. Your promise is called an IOU. An IOU is just what it sounds like — "I owe you." It can help you and your friend re-member exactly what you promised. If you put it in writing, and if you pay your friend back, you won't have any disagreements later — at least not about the money you borrowed.

often take twenty-five or thirty years to pay for a house by taking out a loan and pledging their house to the bank. This pledge is called a mortgage.

# Plastic Money

You can borrow money on the spur of the moment by using a credit card. Banks give people credit cards so they can go to a store or restaurant and buy something even if they don't have cash. It's like an instant loan from the bank.

If you look at a credit card, you will see a raised name and a number. When a salesperson runs one of your parents' credit cards through a machine, the name and number make an impression of the bill. Your parent then signs the paper as a promise to pay the amount later. A copy of this paper is then sent to the credit card company.

Each month, your parents receive a bill that tells them how much money they owe. If they don't pay the full amount, the credit card company charges them interest — just as the bank does when someone borrows money.

## Debtors' Prison

You might lose a friend if you don't pay someone the money you owe. If grown-ups don't pay back money they owe, the bank can take their car or other possessions. In the old days, however, people were sent to jail if they couldn't pay their debts (the money they owed). These jails were called debtors' prisons.

# You Bet Your Bottom Dollar

**P**ockets bulging with bills! Hundreds of coins tumbling into your hat! Millions of dollars! It could be yours — if you hit the jackpot.

Tempted? It's hard to resist the temptation to get rich quick. People around the world gamble — their pulses race with the thrill of uncertainty and the risk of losing. They will bet on almost anything — on the day a child will be born, whether the groundhog will see its shadow on February 2, or on the outcome of an election. Some folks bet on games of chance — lotteries, bingo, card games, dice, coin tosses, and wheels of fortune.

People bet on sports. In Japan, they like to bet on bicycle races. The English are avid gamblers on soccer games. Americans and Canadians bet on boxing

matches and horse races. Horse racing! More people go to horse races than to all the professional football, basketball, and baseball games combined.

Since so many people are willing to gamble, many countries run national lotteries. One of the oldest and richest is the Irish Sweepstakes. The District of Columbia and about thirty states in the U.S.A. as well as five Canadian provinces raise millions of dollars in government-run lotteries. The prizes can be enormous, as much as $100 million, but the chances of winning are slim.

Lotteries are one way for governments to raise money to pay their expenses. In the United States, the lotteries sold $18.5 billion worth of tickets in 1989; the states kept $7.3 billion. In Canada, the provinces sold $3.8 billion in tickets, and kept $1.4 billion. The rest of the money was paid to a handful of winners.

## Uneven Odds

Gambling is done in a thousand ways, but you're always playing against the odds. The *odds* are your chances of winning. The chances of winning the grand prize in a government lottery are one in 5,200,000; the chances of making money at the racetrack are one in 100; the chances of getting a royal flush (ace, king, queen, jack, and ten in one suit) in poker are one in 649,734. The chances of getting hit by lightning during a storm are even better — one in 600,000. And you know how likely that is!

# The Soon To Be Valuable

It seems almost everyone collects something. We have found seashells that cave dwellers in France collected forty thousand years ago! Today, people collect dolls, stamps, baseball cards, buttons, comics, matchbook covers, books, salt and pepper shakers, toy soldiers, shells, spoons, glass bottles, and electrical insulators.

# Holy Cow! Batman!

Comic books aren't just kid stuff. In 1988, a dusty, old comic book found in an attic was sold for $35,000. It was the 1938 Detective Comics, No. 27, the first adventure of Batman and Robin. In 1987, a slightly faded copy of the 1939 Marvel Comics, No. 1, the first *Superman* comic, sold for $82,000.

# Hitting a Home Run

The most famous of all baseball cards is the 1910 Honus Wagner, a card that came with packs of Sweet Caporals cigarettes. Wagner, a Hall of Fame shortstop who played with the Pittsburgh Pirates, was a nonsmoker and didn't want to lure kids to tobacco. He demanded his picture be removed, and only a few of his cards escaped destruction.

Like any collectible, baseball cards are only valuable if they're rare. There aren't many cards from the early days of baseball because kids in those days played with their cards by flipping them to the ground. As a collector, your best bet is the rookie cards. You never know who might end up in the Hall of Fame.

# Tinker, Tailor, Soldier, Sailor

**H**ockey's superstar Wayne Gretzky takes home $2.7 million a year — just for playing hockey. Sylvester Stallone can pocket $25 million for acting in one movie. Some family doctors earn around $85,000 a year. A crossing guard makes less than $12,000; a police officer makes $34,000; a bus driver earns $23,000; an airplane pilot $47,000; a pharmacist $38,000, and a worker at a fast-food restaurant $10,000.

Why do some people earn more than others? The stars — baseball players, actors, and singers — have special skills, and thousands of people are willing to pay to see them perform. Airplane pilots must spend three years in aeronautics school before they can fly passenger jets. It takes only a few weeks to become a city bus driver. A pharmacist goes to school for six years after high school; a restaurant worker learns on the job. The salaries most people earn depend on the training and skills needed to do the job and the responsibility the person must shoulder. Often the more serious the consequences of doing the work badly, the more money people are paid to do the job.

**M O N E Y   F U N**

# Choosing a Career

Ask some grown-ups you know what they like about their jobs. Would you like to do those jobs? What jobs would you enjoy? Fire fighter? Actor? Waiter? Newspaper reporter? Can you think of any others?

# A Taxing Tale

**P**eople have had to share their money with their governments since the beginning of civilization. We still do it whenever we pay a tax.

## Kinds of Taxes

What are these things called taxes, and why do we have to pay them? A tax is the money the government collects from us when we work, shop, own a house, get married, drive a car, smoke tobacco — even die. Governments spend some of the money they collect to build schools, roads, parks, and hospitals. They spend some more of the money to care for the poor, to pay the police officers and fire fighters who protect us, and the soldiers and sailors who defend our country. These are things one person or one family or one small group of people couldn't pay for on their own. Governments can buy them because they get a little money from a lot of people.

We pay taxes to the governments of our towns, cities, states or provinces, and nations. There are many kinds of taxes. People with jobs pay *income tax* on the money they earn. Usually, some of the money they've earned is taken from their paycheck by their boss and sent to the government. Once a year, they make sure their boss sent the right amount by completing an *income tax form*. If the right amount wasn't sent, they either send more money or they get some of their money back.

A tax on income is only one kind of tax. In some states and provinces, there is a *sales tax* on things you buy. If you buy a toy or game for $1.00, the clerk may ask you to pay $1.05. The extra five cents is a tax that is sent to the government. There are taxes on gasoline, cigarettes, liquor, and movie tickets. Sometimes when you cross a bridge or drive on a highway, you must pay a *toll*, which is also a kind of tax. People who own houses must pay a tax on their property. We even pay a tax for the right to do some things — we pay a tax for licenses to get married, to drive a car, to own a dog, even to ride a bike. *Tariffs* are taxes on things we buy from other countries.

## Boston Tea Party

People have protested and complained about taxes for as long as rulers and governments have tried to collect them. In 1773, the American colonists got angry about the taxes they had to pay to the British government. England refused to remove a tax on tea that was sent to the colonies, and the colonists refused to pay it. When three tea ships landed in Boston, a group of colonists disguised themselves as Indians, boarded the ships at night, and threw the tea into the harbor.

# Money for Friends

I n Canada and the United States, despite all the government does to help, many people don't get enough food to eat, and some people have no place to live. Money is always needed to protect the environment, to build hospitals, to find cures for diseases, and to send food to children in other countries. Many folks who have enough try to share with people who don't have enough. But instead of just handing a few dollars to a hungry family, these people try to reach as many of those in need as possible.

They use the same idea the government does — they get a little from a lot of people. They use the money to help people — and they don't keep any of the money for themselves. The work these people do is called *charity*.

## When Is a Bank Not a Bank?

Just as people put their money in a money bank, people and companies deposit food in a food bank. But the people who take the food out of the food bank are not the same people who put it in. The food is there for people who would not have enough to eat otherwise.

If you have more than enough to eat, you might take your extra groceries to a food bank, which will give them to a hungry family.

## Can You Help?

Take a look around you. There are a million causes or groups that need your help. Find the one that you like best—then get to work.

Let's say you would like to feed the cats at the local pound. Your goal is to collect a hundred dollars to buy cat food. How on earth can one person get that much money? Easy—have a raffle!

First, you need to think of a good prize, something everyone will want. Maybe it could be a book about cats. Perhaps some-one will donate one for you to give away.

Next, you will need tickets. If you think you can sell two hundred tickets, you will need to charge fifty cents a ticket (50¢ x 200 tickets = $100). Remember to put numbers on them and to write down who buys which ticket.

You'll need to sell your idea every time you sell a ticket. Be ready to answer questions about the reason for the raffle.

The rest is easy. And when you're done, you will feel terrific. And so will all those cats!

# You Are The Economy

**E**very decision you make — to buy a bike instead of skateboard, or to go to a movie or put your money in the bank — affects your country's economy.

## Decisions We Make

Our economy, as confusing and complex as it might seem, is really just the result of the decisions about working, spending, saving, borrowing, and investing that each of us makes every day as we go about our lives. As a nation, too, we must decide how money will be collected and spent — whether to collect income tax or highway tolls, whether to build submarines or hospitals.

These decisions are like pebbles dropping into a pond — the ripples spread beyond our own lives into the world around us. If you and lots of other kids decide to buy bikes, bicycle manufacturers might decide to hire an advertising agency to promote their bikes; the advertising agency might pay an artist to draw the pictures for some billboards. The artist might give some of the money she earns to her child, and the child might spend it on a bike.

their dollar doesn't stretch as far. If they spend less, some businesses will slow down and some people will lose their jobs, plunging the economy into a *recession.*

## A Global Economy

The impact of our decisions spreads beyond the borders of our country. A farmer in Kansas grows wheat that's made into bread in Russia. A child in western Canada plays with a doll made in Korea. Oil from a field in Saudi Arabia becomes fuel for cars in France. Although you can use dollars to shop at your local market, international trade is usually done in the money of the country selling the goods. A car dealer in the United States who buys cars from Japan must pay for the cars with yen he buys at the bank. The number of yen he gets for each dollar is called the *exchange rate.* The rate varies from day to day depending on the demand for the currency. If Americans buy more Japanese products — and more people want yen — the yen will rise in price against the dollar.

## Ups and Downs

During times when consumers are spending and businesses are growing, the economy is said to be booming. Sometimes businesses can't keep up with consumer demand and prices start to climb — a condition called *inflation.* Rising prices make it harder for people to buy what they need —

# PENNY-WISE

Here we are at the end of our book. We hope we have left you with a better understanding of the world of money. If we have, then you also have a better understanding of your world, and you possess an important tool. Just as a hammer lets you build a house or a bench, money helps you build your life of work and play.

## Answers to questions

Page 10:
The hatmaker will have to make four trades.
Page 41:
At the end of ten years you will have $25.93.